CHESHAM
A Pictorial History

Market Square, 1921

CHESHAM
A Pictorial History

Julian Hunt

Phillimore

1997

Published by
PHILLIMORE & CO. LTD.
Shopwyke Manor Barn, Chichester, West Sussex
in association with
Buckinghamshire County Council
Library, Information, Museum and Archive Services

ISBN 1 86077 058 4

Printed and bound in Great Britain by
BIDDLES LTD.
Guildford, Surrey

List of Illustrations

Frontispiece: Market Square, 1921

Acknowledgements

The photographs used in this book were chosen not to show Chesham in an attractive light but to illustrate aspects of the town's history which I wished to emphasise. The majority of the photographs are from the County Records and Local Studies Service in Aylesbury or from Chesham Library. Several photographs of old houses and farm-steads come from the Royal Commission on Historical Monuments at Swindon (numbers 15, 33, 37, 52, 62, 64-5, 75, 83-7, 123, 137). Some of the most significant images, particularly of Chesham's industrial history, come from the collection of Ray East of Chesham. These are numbered 4-8, 10, 13, 34, 42-4, 50, 101, 103, 107, 111, 115, 120-2, 125, 131, 136, 140, 144-9, 152, 155, 158-61, 167, 169-72. James Venn of Great Missenden contributed several of his own and his friend Stanley Freese's photographs of local mills. These comprise 11, 14-15, 17-19, 21, 23, 28, 56, 117-18, 124, 132-3, 150, 156-7, 168. Two fine railway photographs are by Mr. G.C. Farnell (134-5). Where suitable illustrations were not available, new photographs were taken by Alan Petford (numbers 95, 97) and by myself (26, 66-7, 112, 142, 153).

Particular thanks go to Arnold Baines for good conversation, constructive criticism and early proof reading; to Ray East for finding the right images and helping to caption his photographs; and to Clive Foxell for advice on railway history. Errors which remain in the text are, however, entirely my own responsibility.

Introduction

Before its division into new parishes in 1897, Chesham was by far the largest parish in Buckinghamshire, comprising 12,746 acres. For agricultural and administrative convenience, Great Chesham was divided into the township of Chesham and the hamlets of Hundridge, Chartridge, Asheridge, Bellingdon, Ashley Green, Botley, Latimer and Waterside. Chesham was once even larger, for it is clear that Chesham Bois (910 acres) and Chenies (1,759 acres) were amongst the five estates called Cestreham in Domesday Book.

The land rises from about 275 feet above sea level in the Chess Valley at Latimer to about 600 feet on the Chiltern plateau beyond Chartridge. The town is situated where several now dry valleys converge. Water issues out of springs at Frogmoor in Pednor Bottom on the north west, at Halfway House on the west and at Higham Mead to the north. The three streams run through or beneath the streets before joining to form a river once powerful enough to turn several water mills and still pure enough to grow watercress. Although Chesham was a market town from medieval times, it was not on a through route and its market attracted only the products of the town and its hamlets. The only good road was along the Chess Valley towards London, the destination of the agricultural surplus of the parish and the products of its textile, leather, paper and wooden-ware industries.

Chesham's boundaries were probably set out in the middle-Saxon period when the Chilterns were sparsely populated. Settlement naturally began in those places where a reliable supply of water was available. The earliest recorded form of the place name, Ceasteleshamm, suggests a heap of stones beside a water meadow. No fortified position has been found and it is likely that the name refers to a stone circle marking a place of worship or assembly. The unusually large pudding stones visible in the foundations of St Mary's Church may be evidence of such an ancient meeting place.

The ridges between the dry valleys to the west and north of the town and the plateau to the east provided well drained land suitable for arable farming. The names of several ridges, Hundridge, Chartridge, and Bellingdon, probably derive from Saxon landholders called Hunda, Caerda, and Bella, although the surviving field name Wickeridge or Vicarage suggests that Bellingdon may once have had a purely topographical name. Asheridge, Ashley Green and Hawridge, or 'hawk ridge' (geographically in the orbit of Chesham but appropriated at an early date as hill pasture for the parish of Marsworth) are topographical, but Botley must refer to a clearing belonging to an individual called Botta. The wooded areas at the heads of the valleys would be in process of clearance to provide pasture for cattle and sheep. Some woodland would be preserved for fuel and building materials and for keeping pigs.

The whole parish of Chesham may have been a royal estate in Saxon times. It probably belonged to King Edwy, who ruled England from 955 to 957 when the Mercians revolted because he had made too many gifts of land to his favourites. The realm was reunited under his brother Edgar in 959. Edwy's unjustly divorced wife Elgiva had received a substantial settlement including at least part of the Chesham estate. In a will dated to about 970 she left this land, subject to Edgar's approval, to the Abbey of Abingdon. Following the anti-monastic reaction, the estate may have reverted to the Crown, for in 1066 the largest estate in Chesham belonged to Brictric, a man of Queen Edith, whilst the Queen held another large estate at Chesham in her own right. Further land in Chesham was held by men of Earl Harold and his brother Leofwine. These landlords would have had many tenants but at least six of them were freeholders who could sell their land. The five Chesham estates were taxed at the round figure of 15 hides (the hide being a Saxon taxation measure originally equivalent to a family holding of about 120 acres of arable land). This was a gross under-assessment for an area with such agricultural potential. The concession probably dated back to Elgiva's time and was probably intended to assist in the development of the high Chilterns in which the penal slaves liberated by her will were certainly engaged.

Domesday Book

The division of Chesham into several estates continued after the Norman Conquest. As William regarded himself as the lawful successor to King Edward, he was obliged to leave Edward's widow Edith in possession of her own land at Chesham, which was assessed at four hides. This estate included a mill worth 6s. 8d. and enough woodland to support 800 pigs, suggesting that it extended from the river to the uplands beyond the dry valleys. It may however have been a portfolio of land scattered over the whole parish. This estate descended to a family named Sifrewast who, in the 12th century, gave their rights to nominate a priest at Chesham and to collect the tithes (a tenth of each tenant's crop given to the church) to the Abbey of St Mary de Pre in Leicester. The Sifrewast manor became known as Chesham Bury and their manor house, Bury Hill House, stood to the north of St Mary's Church. The family gave their corn mill on the Chess to the Abbey of Missenden; it thus became known as Canons' Mill, later Cannon Mill.

William gave the larger 8½-hide estate which had belonged to Brictric, a man of Edith, to Hugh de Bolbec, whose principal holding in Buckinghamshire was at Whitchurch. Bolbec Castle is still a significant landscape feature just south of the road from Whitchurch to Oving. The Bolbecs' estates descended to the Earls of Oxford who gave their rights to appoint a priest at Chesham and to collect the tithes there to the Abbey of Woburn. They secured a charter to hold a weekly market and a three-day fair at Chesham in 1257, and in 1329 gained the right to hold the view of frankpledge, a local court which their own tenants and those of the other Chesham estates were obliged to attend. Their mill, highly valued at 10s. in 1086, became known as Lord's Mill as all their tenants had to grind their corn there. Their estate was later known as the manor of Chesham Higham.

William gave the land of Harold and Leofwine, valued at 1½ hides, to his half-brother Odo, Bishop of Bayeux. This land later descended to a family named Bois and became a separate chapelry and then the parish of Chesham Bois. The two mills on the estate may have been on the sites of the later corn mill called Amy Mill and the fulling mill named Bois Mill. Although the Bois family secured the right to appoint a priest to the church on their estate, the tithes were still payable to the Abbey of St Mary de Pre, Leicester.

Domesday Book mentions two further estates in Chesham, valued at only half a hide each. One of these belonged before the Conquest to a freeholder called Epy, a man of Brictric. In 1086 it was held by Turstin Mantel whose estate in neighbouring Amersham is still called Mantles Green. The pre-conquest owner of the other estate is not named, but in 1086, Roger held the land under Odo, Bishop of Bayeux. These two estates could well represent Latimer and Chenies which shared the topographical name of Isenhampstead, meaning a homestead by an iron-bearing spring or stream. The element 'Isene' may be an earlier name of the river Chess, which does drain several chalybeate springs. Isenhampstead Chenies took its manorial name from the Cheyne family, owners from the 13th century, whilst Isenhampstead Latimers derives the second part of its name from the family who acquired it in the 14th century. Their surname Latimer derived from 'latiner', an interpreter. Chenies established a separate identity and its chapel became a parish church whilst Latimer remained a hamlet whose chapel was subordinate to St Mary's, Chesham. The fact that Latimer's tithes remained payable to the priest, who was therefore technically a rector, show that it had an early identity separate from the principal Chesham manors whose tithes were given to monastic houses.

Sometime after Domesday, further manors were created by gifts of land from the overlords to favoured tenants. Blackwell Hall manor originated in a grant of land by the lord of the manor of Chesham Bury. At Hundridge, the Le Broc family had become freeholders by the 12th century but would still have had to attend the manorial court of Chesham Higham. They were influential enough to build their own chapel at Hundridge, served by Woburn Abbey. The building ceased to be used for worship at the Dissolution but has survived as a domestic building. Grove was another freehold manor, but the owner was obliged to pay a chief rent of 13s. 4d. a year to the lord of Chesham Higham; its remarkable double moat may well have been a status symbol.

Agriculture

Domesday Book gives a very clear description of the agricultural organisation of Chesham. Adding together the figures for all the five estates called Cestreham, we find that the land was held by 29 tenant farmers and 16 smallholders who controlled 14 unfree labourers. Between them they had 26 ploughs but there was only sufficient meadow land to feed the oxen for 21 ploughs; there must therefore have been some permanent pasture. The woodland supported 1,650 pigs and some timber from the largest estate was earmarked for making ploughshares, the earliest evidence of a manufacturing industry. There were no fewer than four water-powered corn mills; it is a reasonable hypothesis that the flour from all these mills was more than the locals themselves needed and that the surplus was already intended for the London market.

Successive owners of these Domesday estates and their tenants in the town and its hamlets held much of their land in common. A farmer living in the town might hold strips of land in large arable fields such as Church Field, Broad Field and Town Field. Farmers in the hamlet of Bellingdon shared fields on either side of the ridge and referred to their strips as 'parcels of arable land' in common fields called Wood Field, Flaxfield, Netherfield and Stony Field. Historians are divided as to the antiquity and origin of these common fields. It is highly probable that they predate the Norman Conquest and result from an agreed manorial policy of allocating newly cultivated land fairly between tenants. Since most landlords held land scattered in the fields of both the town and its hamlets, it seems likely that their tenants within the town were encouraged to cultivate the surrounding land in common and only later to set up individual farms on the higher ground. Evidence of common fields survives in Chesham, where the Cottage Hospital is built on one of the strips or slipes in the Town Field, and in the area of land called White Hawridge, where steep banks still divide cultivation terraces in the common field.

Enclosure

Whilst the enclosure of most Midland parishes was a sudden transformation brought about by an Act of Parliament and an Enclosure Award, the conversion of Chesham's common arable fields to separate closes was a long process effected by the agreement of the farmers in each hamlet. Some enclosure in Chesham was noted by a commission in 1517 when the government was alarmed by the numbers of labourers displaced from the land. Enclosure took centuries to complete; because the common fields were small and numerous, they could only be tackled piecemeal. A Board of Agriculture report of 1795 found only 300 acres in Chesham still in common fields. By 1843, when the tithe map was drawn up, parts of Town Field and White Hawridge were still held in 'acre pieces' used for arable farming. The extent of the old common fields can however be detected elsewhere by the survival of hedged strips and the recurrence of the same field names in the lists of closes belonging to neighbouring farms.

In only one part of Chesham was an Act of Parliament needed to promote enclosure. Most of Hyde Heath was enclosed in 1807 under the Timber Act of 1755-6, although two greens survived. Despite enclosure, the increased efficiency of Chesham's farms and the drift to new industrial jobs in the town, there were still over 450 agricultural labourers in the parish in 1851.

Tithes

Right up until the 1840s, the farmers of Chesham were obliged to give a 'tithe' or tenth of their produce to the church. Had a priest at Chesham received the 'great tithes' (a tenth of the crops) he would have had a very good income and the status of a rector. In fact the two principal landlords had given their rights to collect the great tithes and to nominate a priest to two different abbeys, Woburn in Bedfordshire and St Mary de Pre in Leicester. Each abbot appointed a vicar whose income was to be the 'small tithes' from the farms on the respective manors, comprising the tenth of milk produced and the tenth animal born. The two vicars worked as a team in the one church, but increasingly the abbots and, after the Dissolution, their lay successors agreed on a single candidate who could better support himself on the whole of the small tithes, which were notoriously difficult to collect.

The tithes or 'rectory' of Chesham Woburn descended to the Dukes of Bedford, whose tenant in the estate farm at Hyde Heath would act as their agent. Hyde House remained the manor house of Chesham Woburn rectory until the tithes were bought out by the landowners. In the 18th century the rectory of Chesham Leicester was acquired by the Skottowe family, who sold their right to appoint a vicar to the Duke of Bedford by 1767 but retained their half of the great tithes. They lived at the mansion called Bury Hill House, sometimes called the Upper Parsonage or Rectory, which stood to the north of the church and was purchased and demolished by William Lowndes of the Bury in 1802. The site is now part of Lowndes Park. Following the Tithe Redemption Act of 1836, all tithes were to be converted into money payments charged on land according to its extent and quality. A detailed map of Chesham was prepared and the name of the owner, occupier and tithe owner of every plot of land was entered in a ledger. All the sums of money involved had been paid off by 1995, but the beautiful map, giving a name to almost every field and copse, survives in the County Record Office in Aylesbury.

Corn Mills

Chesham's primary industry in medieval times must have been the production of flour for sale on the London market. The Chess powered four mills at Domesday to which at least three more were added before some sites were used to power other processes. A survey down the river starts with Amy Mill, whose mill pond survives in the Meades Water Gardens alongside the Amersham Road. Until the boundary changes of 1934 the mill was within Chesham Bois parish. It is first mentioned in the parish registers in 1616 when John Dell of Amee Mill is buried. The water mill was replaced by a steam-powered corn mill built on the other side of the Amersham Road about 1845. The new mill was at one time called Bois Steam Mill, leading to confusion with the old fulling mill called Bois Mill near Latimer. There is no evidence that Amy Mill was ever a fulling mill.

The next mill on the river was Lord's Mill, the mill pond created in Saxon times by diverting the Chess. The mill was valued at 10s. in Domesday Book and served the tenants of Chesham Higham manor for centuries. Lord's Mill was the last corn mill to operate on the Chess. It was demolished in 1988, but the mill house survives.

Further downstream was Cannon Mill, the name acquired when it belonged to the canons of Missenden Abbey. It was last worked in the 1930s and was demolished about 1960. Next was Weirhouse Mill, which was partially converted to a paper mill in the 18th century. It reverted to corn milling in 1858 and operated until the 1940s. Blackwell Hall manor had its own corn mill which was converted to a paper mill in 1774 and demolished about 1860.

From its name, it can be assumed that Bois Mill was originally the principal corn mill for Chesham Bois. By the 16th century it had been converted into a fulling mill, where huge wooden fulling stocks lifted by the water wheel felted locally woven cloth. From 1769 to 1865 the mill was used for the manufacture of paper. Most of the buildings were removed about 1900, but the mill house remains. There is no trace of any mill which might have served the tenants of Latimer, but Chenies Mill, converted to a paper mill by the 1740s, reverted to corn milling in the 1850s, and continued until the 1930s.

Millers and mealmen appear regularly in Chesham parish registers. The occupation is found seven times between 1538-1636 and 19 times between 1637-1730. It is difficult to compare the mills but the numbers employed and the productivity of Buckinghamshire corn mills in 1798 are given in the *Posse Comitatus*, a list of the military potential of the county. The following information on mills has been compiled from this source:

Mill	Occupier	Weekly Production	Horses	Wagons	Carts
Amy	Thomas Wright	20 quarters			2
Lord's	James Tuffnell	40 sacks	7	2	2
Cannons	John Bailey	200 sacks	7	2	3
Weirhouse	Aaron Moody	70 sacks	1		1

Cloth-making

A town which milled corn for the London market was likely to turn some of its water-wheels over to other industrial purposes. The domestic and overseas demand for English cloth meant that most market towns had their weavers and clothworkers, but Chesham had the advantage of a large-scale cloth finishing mill at Chesham Bois, and the town's clothiers were only one day's pack-horse journey from the great cloth market at Blackwell Hall, near London's Guildhall. Weavers, clothworkers, and dyers are referred to 23 times in Chesham's parish registers from 1538-1636. Sixteen wills of Chesham weavers and clothiers were proved in the Archdeaconry Court of Buckingham prior to 1660, the earliest being Ralph Sutton of Chesham, weaver in 1558. Owing to the shortage of coinage in the 17th century, several Chesham merchants issued their own tokens, including a clothier named Richard Amond whose token bore the Clothworkers' arms. A fulling mill for finishing cloth is first mentioned in 1592 in the will of John Carter of Chesham Bois, fuller. He bequeaths to his wife Elizabeth 'all the term and residue of the years mentioned in my lease of the mill that shall be then unexpired'. A kinsman, Daniel Carter of Chesham, dyer, made his will 4 January 1648, leaving to his son Benjamin 'all my dyeing vessels belonging to my dyehouse being three furnaces in my dyehouse and more one small furnace near unto the kitchen and six old vats and two leaden cisterns and all other implements belonging to the dying vessels'. He also left Benjamin his 'great sheers belonging to my shop with all my handles belonging to the dressing of cloth with two shear boards and three pair of tenters standing in the common field commonly called by the name of Town Field and my hot press'. Clothworkers, dyers, fullers, shearmen, shear grinders, spinning masters, stock-card makers, and wadmal (coarse cloth) weavers, together numbering 146, far exceed any other group of tradesmen listed in Chesham's parish registers from 1637-1730. Shoemakers, the next largest group, are mentioned only 52 times.

The whole of a clothier's family might be involved in the trade, with women and children hand-carding wool and spinning yarn in the house, and father, sons and journeymen weavers working at hand-looms upstairs or in a workshop. The fullers washed and felted the cloth under heavy wooden fulling stocks, lifted and dropped by cams on the waterwheel shaft; croppers put the cloth on shear-boards and cut off loose fibres with great shears; and dyers coloured the cloth with woad before hanging it to dry on tenters which fixed the dimensions of the pieces.

The Chesham woollen industry contracted in the early 18th century when the Yorkshire woollen industry was expanding rapidly and dominating the market for fine broadcloths. The trade had disappeared from the town before the first carding and spinning mills appeared in Yorkshire and almost 100 years before the appearance of the power-loom. The dyer's strip of land in the Town Field was used to grow corn again and the fulling stocks at the mill were converted to grind rags for paper making.

Paper-making

Few cities in the world had as big an appetite for paper as London had. Many mills in the Buckinghamshire and Hertfordshire Chilterns were turned over to paper manufacture in the 17th century with finance from London rag merchants and stationers, but it was not until the middle of the 18th century that some of the mills in the Chess Valley were converted. George Mowdray, paper maker, the tenant of Weirhouse Mill at Waterside, insured the buildings in 1768; George Street of Bucklersbury, London, stationer, bought Blackwell Hall Mill in 1774; Richard Loosely leased the old fulling mill at Chesham Bois from the Duke of Bedford in 1769, raising a £400 mortgage on the premises from a London rag merchant named Samuel Hunter; and John Dodd, miller and paper maker, insured his mill at Chenies in 1763. According to the *Posse Comitatus*, the list of men liable for military service in 1798, there were 14 paper makers in Waterside, nine in Chesham Bois and 11 in Chenies, but only one is listed in the town itself.

These mills used their water power to raise wooden stampers which broke up rags brought from London. In the 18th century rag engines were introduced in which rags were ground against fixed knives. The fibres were then mixed with chemicals in a large vat to form a pulp. In the earlier factories, the paper maker used a wire sieve to draw from the vat sufficient pulp to form a sheet of paper. It was the wires of the paper mould which left the faint lines which characterise hand-made paper.

Henry Brewer of Chesham Bois, a wire worker and paper mould maker, was made bankrupt in October 1812. In about 1800, two London stationers named Fourdrinier developed a process of drawing off a continuous film of pulp from the vat and pressing the paper between rollers before winding it on to a drum. The new machine was first used in about 1800 at their mill at Frogmoor near Hemel Hempstead but other manufacturers were soon licensed to operate similar machines. A Fourdrinier machine was erected in 1807 by Richard Elliott at the old fulling mill in Chesham Bois and another was installed by John Allnutt further upstream at Weir House Mill in 1819.

The Chess Valley paper mills were not affected by the Swing riots which resulted in the destruction of much of the machinery in the High Wycombe paper mills. Nonetheless, they succumbed to rationalisation of the industry and were all closed down in the mid-19th century. The paper machinery was removed from Weir House Mill in 1858 and the mill reverted to grinding corn, but the characteristic white boarding of the drying sheds is visible even today. Blackwell Hall Mill, described in an 1830 directory as operated by George Stevens 'on a very large scale', had extensive machinery which is described in an inventory of 1846, soon after the mill was bought and closed down by the Cavendish family of Latimer. There is no trace of this mill today. The mill at Chesham Bois, probably the last to operate as a paper mill, was bought and closed down by the Cavendish family in 1865, but the fine miller's house remains. The Dodd family mill at Chenies reverted to corn milling in 1849.

Lace-making

The production of bone lace was introduced into Buckinghamshire during the 16th century, often as a means of employing the poor. The local draper or lace buyer acted as a wholesaler, supplying linen thread and patterns to outworkers who each week received the value of their lace less the cost of the thread. The lace buyers attended the Monday lace market at the *Bull and Mouth* in St Martin's by Aldersgate, or the Tuesday market at the *George Inn*, Aldersgate Street. The Chesham and Amersham lace buyers were known to specialise in black lace, but it is difficult to gauge the volume of the trade. Despite being seen in 1792 as the principal occupation of the town, the lace industry left behind no factories or account books; the lace-maker required only a pillow stuffed with straw, a leather pattern through which pins were inserted to dictate the style, and a set of bobbins (originally made of bone) with which to keep the threads under tension. The Chesham parish registers between 1637 and 1730 list eight lace buyers, three male lace-makers and one pattern maker. The 1792 directory lists four lace buyers, Thomas Creed, Thomas Plastow, George Sutthery and Thomas Treacher. The hundreds of women and children whom each lace buyer employed are nowhere listed until the mid-19th century. By then the trade was in terminal decline, the work having migrated to Nottingham where the lace-making process had been successfully mechanised. In 1851 there were only 76 lace-makers and one lace buyer in Chesham.

Straw-plaiting

Chesham responded to the collapse of the market for hand-made lace by embracing another domestic industry. The growing fashion for straw bonnets in the late 18th century had prompted many families in the agricultural districts to the north west of London to supplement their income by weaving split straw into the plait used by the bonnet makers. As the wages paid to straw plaiters outstripped those of the lace-makers, the younger women, the children, and even some men learnt the new trade. By 1830, Chesham lace buyers were also dealing in straw plait and a plait market was held each Saturday. *Kelly's Directory* in 1847 reported that 'straw plait is also manufactured to a large extent' and noted the Saturday market for straw and tuscan plaits. Tuscan plait was a particularly fine plait manufactured from straw specially imported from Italy. In 1851 there were over 700 plait makers in Chesham and its hamlets. The plaiters were predominantly the wives and daughters of shoemakers and agricultural labourers. The trade was financed by nine straw plait dealers (three of whom were from one family named Reading) and there was a straw plait school in Waterside run by Milicent Mayo, the wife of a wood turner. Although there were 25 straw bonnet makers, most of the product was purchased by the hat manufacturers of Luton and Dunstable which towns had become the centre of the trade.

Silk-spinning

The spinning and weaving of silk was another trade introduced into several Buckinghamshire towns in order to employ those who would otherwise have been a burden on the poor rates. The mill at Tring is still standing but the silk weaving factory built in 1833 at Aylesbury has long since disappeared. According to a government return of 1838, the silk spinning mill recently built at Waterside was steam driven. It was run by Thomas Rock Shute, who owned the larger Rookery Silk Mill in Watford. By 1851, he was employing 38 men and 86 women at the mill. In the 1856 Parliamentary return, two Buckinghamshire silk spinning mills are mentioned, both powered by steam, having 4,440 spindles between them. A treaty with France in 1860 allowed the import of superior French silks duty free and many of the small silk mills were forced to close; the mill at Chesham is last mentioned in the 1864 trade directory. The building, later used by the Royal Bucks Laundry, was demolished in the 1970s.

Wooden-Ware Manufacture

The Chiltern woodlands were originally seen by London merchants more as a source of firewood than a hive of local industry. The early parish registers of Chesham show, however, that there was a variety of woodland trades practised here. Between 1538-1730, the following tradesmen are mentioned: 27 turners, 17 sawyers, 16 shovel makers, five broom makers, five chair makers, four spoon makers, two trencher makers and one hoop shaver. Some of the specialists were wealthy enough to leave wills, like William Edmond of Chesham Bois, shovel maker, in 1585 and John Cheeseman of Chesham, trencher maker, in 1661. The 1792 directory places wooden ware third behind lace- and shoemaking in the table of Chesham's industry. The trade was 'considerably large; round-ware, hollow-ware, Tunbridge-ware etc.'. The 1830 directory ranked the trades differently, stating that 'the principal manufacture carried on in Chesham is that of coarse wooden-ware, embracing the making of malt shovels in great numbers'.

The 1851 Census shows that the number of men employed in the wooden-ware industry was far less than that in boot and shoe manufacture, but the following trades were represented in Chesham parish; 34 turners, 18 chair makers, 16 hoop makers, 15 shovel makers, 12 wooden-ware manufacturers, five bowl turners, two butter print makers, two spoon makers, and one tray maker, totalling one hundred and five. It was only in the late 19th century that manufacturers like Nathaniel Reynolds began to employ large numbers of turners and other specialists and to operate steam saw-mills and workshops such as his Prospect Works at Waterside. William Wright & Son's General Steam Saw-Mills in Water Lane occupied the site of a small water mill which once ground bark for the nearby tannery. Several firms like James East & Sons and Thomas Wright & Son built new premises in the growing industrial suburb of Newtown. After the Second World War, these family firms failed to compete with cheap imports of wooden ware from countries with abundant timber and cheap labour and most went out of business in the 1960s.

Brush-making

The production of large wooden tools like malt shovels resulted in huge quantities of offcuts which could be fashioned into other useful products. A manufacturer named Robert Webb is credited with setting up the first factory in Chesham to make brush backs in 1829. His example was followed by others and machinery was evolved to turn the manufacture of brushes by hand into a mass production business. Webb's moved their factory from Broadway to new premises in Townsend Road. Many other brush manufacturers like George Hawes also built new factories in Newtown, providing employment for large numbers of men and women. George Hawes' works in Higham Road became Beechwoods Ltd., one of the best known names in brush manufacture nationally. Although Webbs and Beechwoods adopted modern manufacturing methods and synthetic materials, they were forced to merge with other brush manufacturers, whose holding companies had moved production to more favourable localities by the late 1980s.

Boot- and Shoemaking

A directory of 1792 claimed that Chesham's second most important industry was the manufacture of boots. 1,000 pairs were made each week and sold to London wholesalers. The raw material came from Chesham's two tanneries. The principal firm was that of Patrick Hepburn, whose imposing red-brick house still stands on the west side of the High Street. Tanneries require a good supply of water to wash the skins and the tanyard was bounded on the west by the branch of the Chess which runs down from Higham Mead. The other vital resource is the tannin obtained from the bark of trees. William Mead, another Chesham tanner, ran a small water mill in Water Lane grinding bark for the tanyard. His house, now called The Meades, still stands in Germain Street, beside the Town Bridge.

Most shoemakers worked from their own homes and employed few journeymen. By 1851 there were 291 male shoemakers and 85 female shoe binders in Chesham parish. Joseph Barnes, a shoemaker whose premises were on the High Street, was unusual in employing 30 men, women and boys. In the late 19th century, however, several Chesham manufacturers built small factories and installed modern machinery. Instead of the boot being made by one craftsman, the work was divided among several operatives, such as the 'clickers' (men who cut out the uppers), the 'closers' (usually women who machine sewed the uppers), and the riveters (men who secured the upper to the sole).

Two boot and shoe manufacturers feature in an optimistic survey of Chesham industry in the *Examiner* in 1889. James and Edwin Reynolds were then producing 2,000 pairs of boots per week at their works in Blucher Street, and Charles Long was building a new showroom and offices to impress visitors to his factory on the High Street which produced 1,000 pairs per week. The *Examiner* remarked in October 1890 that the boot trade 'could employ from six to eight hundred more hands if they could be found somewhere to live'. The trade declined in the 20th century because Chesham continued to specialise in heavy working-men's boots when the fashion changed to lighter shoes. Giffard Newton & Sons, the firm which began in Church Street in the 1854 and moved to Townsend Road in about 1909, is now the only surviving boot factory.

Chesham in the 20th century

With the growth of cottage industries and subsequent employment in factories, Chesham's population more than doubled in the 19th century, from 3,969 in 1801 to 9,005 in 1901. The cramped yards leading off the main streets became overcrowded and their inhabitants susceptible to disease. The worst epidemic was in 1871 when Dr. Faithorn and the Rev. A.F. Aylward died. Larger towns already had police commissioners or local boards of health to secure better conditions, but Chesham had to wait until 1875 for the formation of the Amersham Rural Sanitary Authority. This body began construction of a reservoir on Alma Road, filled from a bore hole reaching 160 ft. down into the chalk and providing a safe water supply. The Rural Sanitary Authority also began the sewage works at Milk Hall which were completed in 1887. Chesham's own Local Board of Health with nine members, formed in 1884, was superseded in 1894 by the Urban District Council which continued the tradition of town government until 1974.

Chesham Urban District at first extended to the whole of Great Chesham, but in 1897 it was confined to the built-up area of 1,386 acres with a population in 1901 of 7,245. The remainder of the old parish was split into three new civil parishes of Chartridge, Ashley Green and Latimer with populations of 721, 456, and 583 respectively. In 1934 the boundaries were changed again so that the Urban District increased in area to 3,489 acres, taking in parts of Chartridge, Ashley Green, Latimer and Chesham Bois. During the present century, the population has continued to grow as the Urban District built new estates like Pond Park in the 1930s and speculative builers developed housing such as Chessmount and Hilltop in the 1950s and '60s.

Even as the wooden-ware and footwear industries declined, new firms moved to Chesham from London during and after the Second World War. Many built factories on the new industrial estate on Asheridge Road, and brought their workers with them. The population reached 11,433 in 1951.

The Chesham Town Map, agreed between the Urban District and County Councils in 1957, envisaged a population of 20,000, a figure reached in 1971 and hardly exceeded since. It put in place a strict green belt without which the town would undoubtedly have spilled over into the surrounding countryside, especially after the electrification of the railway in 1960. The Town Map also provided for the construction of an inner relief road. Had St Mary's Way not been built in the 1960s, the High Street would have been devastated by road widening and the essential character of this Chiltern industrial town would have been lost for ever.

1 *(above left)* Chesham is surrounded by a series of dry valleys where the soil is clay or gravel overlying chalk. One branch of the river Chess rises in Pednor Mead to the north west of the town where the water which drains through the porous chalk gushes out to form a stream.

3 *(above)* The village of Ceasteleshamm spread around the water meadows and grew in importance as a market centre. By Domesday it was a prosperous agricultural community with 29 tenant farmers, 16 smallholders and 14 labourers. There were 26 ploughs and enough woodland to support 1,650 pigs. Some timber was reserved for making ploughshares, the earliest evidence of a manufacturing industry.

2 *(below left)* The Saxons, who called meadowland next to a river a 'hamm', named the riverside settlement 'Ceasteleshamm', probably referring not to a castle but to a circle of stones arranged for some pagan religious purpose. Several large pudding-stone blocks can still be seen in the foundations of St Mary's Church.

4 Building land on the valley floor was at a premium. The triangle of land between Germain Street and the road to London was filled in by cottages known as Duck Alley, below the Town Bridge.

5 The river Chess is supplied by several chalybeate or iron-bearing springs, once thought to have healing properties. This building with its rose garden was erected on the Amersham Road in 1821 to accommodate those who came to Chesham to take the waters. The place-name element 'isene', meaning iron-bearing, is found in the early names of two settlements further down the river: Isenhampstead Latimer and Isenhampstead Chenies. The river may therefore have had the name 'Isene' before being called the Chesham Stream. The name Chess is a back-formation from the name of the town, and is not found in documents before the 19th century.

6 The pure spring water is ideal for growing watercress for the London market. Here watercress growers are working in an artificially created pool at Waterside.

7 The watercress was taken by cart to London and latterly by lorry to the Metropolitan Railway station. Watercress is still grown in Waterside for local consumption.

8 *(left)* Chesham's farmers were producing enough corn even at Domesday to support four water mills. Amy Mill, situate just south of the town in Chesham Bois parish, may well occupy the site of one of these Domesday mills. It was operated for much of the 19th century by the Rose family but was dismantled before 1900.

9 *(below left)* The fine miller's house, shown here about 1930, was later reduced in size when Amersham Road was widened. It was badly damaged by a lorry and demolished in the 1970s.

10 *(below)* The back door of Amy Mill House opened on to the mill race. The old corn mill must have stood to the left of the footbridge.

11 In 1845, George Rose of Amy Mill was fatally injured by his newly-installed steam-driven machinery. This was in the new mill on the opposite side of the road which became known as Bois Steam Mill and continued to mill corn after the closure of Amy Mill. It was converted into a wooden-ware factory *c*.1900.

12 The Chess was diverted in early medieval times to create the long mill pond for Lord's Mill; this probably gave rise to the hamlet name of Waterside.

13 Lord's Mill is probably on the site of the corn mill valued at 10s. in Domesday Book. Tenants of the manor of Chesham Higham would have been required to grind their corn here. Rebuilt in the 17th century, Lord's Mill had a huge breast-shot water wheel, 25 feet in diameter, facing the town and at right angles to the river. The old water wheel at Lord's Mill was replaced about 1900 by an overshot wheel within the mill. This in turn was replaced by an electric engine.

14 Lord's Mill ceased to grind corn in the 1950s. Despite its status as a listed building, it was left to decay and was demolished in 1988. The mill house with its fine chimneys remains.

15 W.E. Wright and Sons, the corn and coal merchants in Germain Street, ran Lord's Mill from the 1920s until its closure.

16 Housing spread along the Chess to accommodate journeymen millers, clothworkers and paper makers who eventually found employment in the growing hamlet of Waterside.

17 The next mill on the Chess was Cannon Mill, another corn mill, so named because it was on the Chesham estate of the canons of Missenden Abbey. It stood across the stream and was constructed of whitewashed brick with wooden upper walls and a slate roof.

18 Cannon Mill last worked in 1937 and was demolished about 1960.

19 Weirhouse Mill was another corn mill within the hamlet of Waterside. By the 1760s, the mill had been turned over to grinding rags by George Mowdray, of Chesham, paper maker.

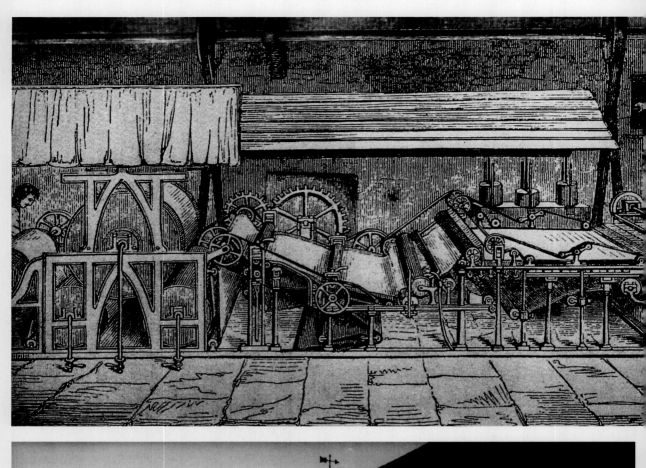

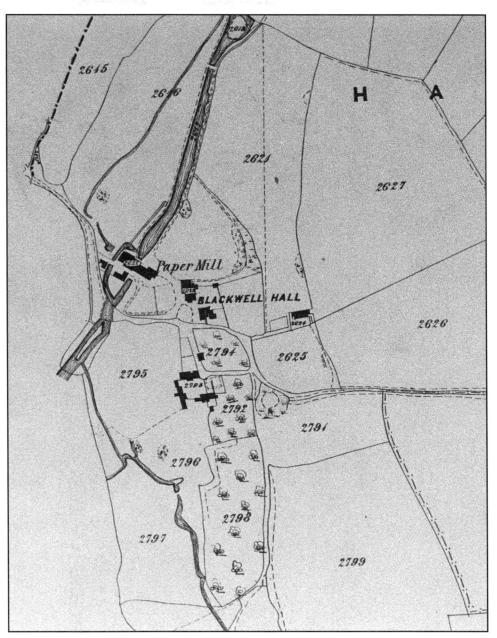

20 *(above left)* In 1819, the proprietor of Weirhouse Mill, John Allnutt, installed a Fourdrinier machine which produced paper on a roll and greatly increased the productivity of the mill. The paper-making machinery was removed in 1858 but the louvre panels, allowing passage of air to dry the paper, are still a feature of the building.

21 *(left)* Weirhouse Mill was converted back to a corn mill in 1858 and run for many years by William Puddephatt. It is now occupied by McMinn Hardware Wholesalers.

22 *(above)* There was a corn mill driven by the Chess on the Blackwell Hall estate. George Street, a London stationer, bought Blackwell Hall Mill in the 1760s and converted it into a paper mill later operated by the Stevens family. *Pigot & Co's Directory* of 1830, referring to Chesham's four paper mills, remarks that 'one of which, belonging to Mr George Stevens, is on a very large scale'. Charles Compton Cavendish of Latimer House bought the mill in 1844 and closed it down soon afterwards. It is clearly shown on the 1843 Tithe Map.

23 Bois Mill was the principal corn mill used by the tenants of Chesham Bois manor. By the 16th century it had been converted into a fulling mill, leased by the Carter family, who finished and dyed locally-woven cloth.

24 Fulling mills used water power to lift wooden fulling hammers which pounded the cloth in troughs of hot water to felt and thicken the cloth. These fulling hammers worked in a mill near Leeds until 1975.

25 During the 16th and 17th centuries, cloth-making was Chesham's major source of income. A Chesham clothier called Richard Amond was wealthy enough to issue his own halfpenny token in 1664 when there was a severe shortage of small change.

26 During the 18th century, the 'Old Fulling Mills' were adapted to grind rags and to produce hand-made paper. In 1789, the mill was leased to Joseph Elliott whose family erected a Fourdrinier paper-making machine there as early as 1807 and ran the mill until the 1850s. Bois Mill was purchased by Lord Chesham in 1865; the mill was dismantled but the fine miller's house remains between the river and the road to Latimer.

27 *(left)* The oldest part of Chesham is the part of Church Street where the road curves over the Nap, around the base of the hill on which St Mary's stands. The jettied building on the right must have been the home of a high status farmer. By 1900 it had become the Old Sun Lodging-house.

29 *(above)* These cottages with fold-down shutters are typical of superior estate cottages. The lodges to the Bury are in the background.

28 *(left)* The Lodging-house was taken down in 1937 and meticulously rebuilt as a country house at Pednor.

30 *(above)* Church Street continues towards the depopulated hamlet of Hundridge as Missenden Road, past these agricultural labourers' cottages.

31 *(above right)* The opening of the Metropolitan Railway in 1889 brought a demand for modern houses in traditional styles. By 1921 the cottages on the north side of Missenden Road had been attractively rebuilt.

32 *(below right)* Development along Missenden Road continued with the building of Chesham Urban District council houses in the late 1940s.

33 These 18th-century cottages in Pednormead End occupy the corner of Church Street and the road to the common arable fields in Pednor Bottom.

34 Pednor Bottom was shared by Hundridge and Chartridge hamlets. The farmers of Chartridge had anciently shaped the north side of the valley into cultivation terraces, one group of which was called Westdean Field. Remains of some of the cultivation terraces can still be seen, especially where the small enclosures suit those wishing to graze horses.

35 The comparatively small Market Square was probably laid out when the Earl of Oxford obtained a charter to hold a market in 1257. The town must already have been the natural centre for the exchange of the agricultural surplus produced in such a large and fertile parish.

36 *(above)* Chesham's farmers would sell their corn in the Market Square, either by the cart-load or, if some suitable building were available, at a corn market where farmers could show samples of their grain to the millers or corn merchants. A market hall is first mentioned in the Quarter Sessions books in 1679.

37 *(above right)* Chesham Town Hall was rebuilt and enlarged in 1856 by Lord Chesham. The upper storey was used for manor courts, petty sessions, public meetings and concerts, and later for the Urban District Council. The space below the arches was intended for a corn exchange and gave shelter to some of the market stalls. When this photograph was taken in 1965, the handsome clock tower and lantern had been removed prior to the demolition of the building.

38 *(below right)* With the demolition of the Town Hall, the Market Square was temporarily opened up to traffic pending pedestrianisation. North-bound vehicles were diverted onto a new ring road called St Mary's Way, whilst south-bound traffic continued to use the High Street.

40 *(right)* The *Crown Hotel* stood at the junction of High Street and the Market Square. Looking from Church Street, we can see through the coach entrance into the stable yard. The hotel was demolished and replaced by a shop *c*.1960.

39 *(below)* What business was not conducted in the Town Hall could be transacted in one of the inns near the Market Square. The *Universal Directory* of 1792 reckoned that the *Red Lion*, the *Nag's Head*, the *George* and the *Crown* were the most reliable. The *Red Lion* stood on the corner of Germain Street until 1937 when it was demolished for road widening.

41 *(below right)* Just off the Market Square in Church Street was the *Golden Ball*, another inn popular with farmers on market day. It now houses a doctors' surgery and the registry office.

42 The *Nag's Head* was another casualty of the 1930s road widening scheme. Its licence was transferred to the adjoining *Red Lion*.

43 Cattle and sheep were sold in the Market Square, but by 1905, the sheep market was held at the *Nag's Head* yard in Red Lion Street.

44 The auctioneers F.E. Howard & Son rented the *Nag's Head* yard from Wellers, the Amersham brewers. Their last sheep market was held there in 1930.

45 The *George Hotel* at the Market Square end of High Street is the only one of the commercial inns to survive to the present day. It was the starting point for the London coach, and later for the horse buses which met the trains at Watford and Berkhamsted.

46 The High Street has some of the character of a planned medieval town but its development was constrained by the river and the steep hillside. The houses on the east side were probably built on strips of arable land in a common field called Dungrove or Town Field, previously cultivated by farmers living in the older part of the town.

47 The buildings along the west side of the High Street are built on a long culvert over a stream which rises to the north of the town at Higham Mead and joins the other headwaters of the Chess just below the Market Square.

48 The cottages in Lum's Yard on the west of High Street are built directly over the culverted stream.

49 The building of houses along the bank of the river to form the High Street connected Chesham to a sub-settlement around a triangular green called Pillory Green. The road here became known as the 'Broadway'. This view from the 1880s looks south along the High Street.

50 The water from Higham Mead passed under the road from Chartridge, originally known as Bridge Street, and ran in front of the houses to the left of this picture. The faded photograph is again from the 1880s.

51 By the early 1900s many of the buildings in the Broadway had been replaced. The Broadway Baptist Chapel, rebuilt in 1902, towers over the neighbouring *Star Inn*.

52 The *Star Inn* stood at the foot of Bridge Street, which was renamed Blucher Street after the Prussian general Gerhard von Blucher who came to Wellington's aid at the Battle of Waterloo.

53 Blucher Street was once a narrow lane leading towards the hamlet of Chartridge. It has been destroyed by the building of the ring road, with only 1 Blucher Street left standing.

54 The market charter of 1257 included the right to hold a three-day annual fair either side of Assumption Day. This was replaced by fairs held on 21 April, 22 July and 28 September, the latter being the hiring fair when farm servants were taken on for the year. The fairs were held in the Broadway until 1938, but since the Second World War the fairs have been held on the Moor.

55 As development continued, the road to the north of the Broadway was urbanised and also became known as High Street. A comparison with the neighbouring market town of Amersham, with its broad thoroughfare extending the length of the town, suggests that Chesham's narrow High Street is the result of piecemeal building rather than medieval planning.

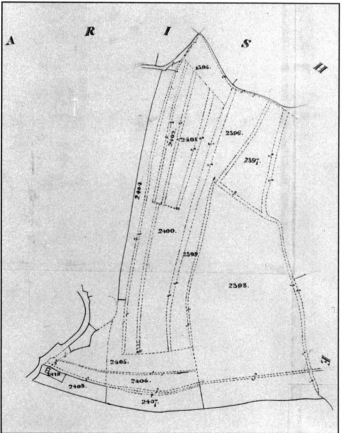

56 Much of the farmland encroached upon by the growing town had been part of a large common field east of the High Street called Dungrove Field. Each farmer in the town would have had strips of arable land in this and other common arable fields such as the Church Field. When one common field was growing wheat, another would have a crop of peas or beans and a third would be fallow. By purchase and exchange, some farmers were able to consolidate large holdings in a common field and make large hedged enclosures. Dungrove Farm was built on land accumulated as part of this process.

57 Dungrove Field was also known as the Town Field, a name now given to the part of the town to the east of Red Lion Street. The surveyor who drew up the tithe map of 1843 made this detailed plan of the remaining strips in the Town Field, drawn at a scale large enough to insert numbers referring to the name and ownership of each narrow plot. Plot 2400 was arable land belonging to William Lowndes and occupied by John Smith. It was named Clever Piece and measured 1 acre, 3 roods and 32 perches.

58 The Cottage Hospital was built on Clever Piece in the Town Field in 1869.

59 The road north out of the town towards Chesham Vale was not built up until the late 19th century. Its successive parts became known as Broad Street, Berkhampstead Road and Vale Road. The police station was built here in 1861 directly opposite the aptly named Townsend Road.

60 Development continued along Berkhampstead Road in the early 20th century. Britannia Road is named after George Barnes' Britannia Boot and Shoe Factory which was in Addison Road behind the trees on the left.

61 At the *Nashleigh Arms*, the road to Berkhamsted turns right up Nashleigh Hill. Straight on is Vale Road which runs along the bottom of one of Chesham's dry valleys dividing the upland hamlet of Bellingdon on the west from Ashley Green on the east. In periods of heavy rainfall such as 1903, when the annual total was 40 inches, the usually dry valley could become a river.

62 Nashleigh Farm, shown here in 1911, is typical of the isolated farmsteads in Ashley Green, one of Chesham's eight hamlets. Built in the 16th or early 17th century, it exhibits the wealth of the Chiltern cereal producer with ready access to local corn mills and the London markets.

63 Nashleigh Farm extended over 91 acres in 1839, most of the land being arable. The photograph of the farmyard was taken in 1907.

64 Vale Farm is in Bellingdon hamlet. Much of the land in the Vale and on the Bellingdon ridge was organised on the medieval open-field principle. There were many common arable fields along the ridge and only by purchase and exchange of strips in these fields did a farm like Vale Farm acquire land in one block.

65 In 1843, James Field, the occupier of Vale Farm, had part of his land at White Hawridge, near the *Black Horse Inn*, where several farmers still had strips of arable land intermixed in the same field.

66 The strips of arable land formed cultivation terraces which are clearly visible on the hillside at White Hawridge, where steep banks and overgrown hedges mark each plot of land. Slight ridges in the field in the foreground remain where further hedge banks have been ploughed out.

67 Each strip at White Hawridge measures about one acre and the height of the hedge banks separating them is about twelve feet. This terrace is now used for grazing horses but in 1843 it was a plot of arable land called Acre Piece numbered 1463 on the tithe map.

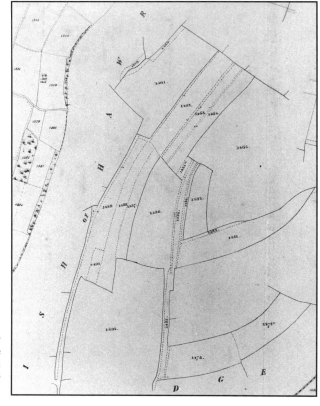

68 White Hawridge common field was only partially enclosed by 1843 when the tithe award was made. The surveyor drew a detailed plan of the remaining cultivation strips in the margin of the tithe map. Note how the strips follow the contours of the hill.

69 In a system of common arable farming, not only was the land of each tenant farmer intermixed with that of his neighbour, but the holdings of Chesham's two principal lords of the manor were also scattered over the whole parish. The largest of the five manors called Cestreham in Domesday Book descended to the Earls of Oxford and was purchased in 1615 by the Cavendish family of Chatsworth in Derbyshire. Their descendants, the Lords Chesham, remained lords of the manor until this century and occupied the great house at Latimer.

70 Latimer House was rebuilt in the 1830s by Charles Compton Cavendish, later Lord Chesham. The architect was Edward Blore and a mock-Tudor style was chosen. The house is now a management training centre belonging to the accountants Coopers and Lybrand. The arms of the Cavendish family can still be seen over the east doorway.

71 The Church of St Mary Magdalene at Latimer was originally a chapelry under St Mary's Church. It was rebuilt by the Cavendish family in 1841, again using the architect Edward Blore.

72 This obelisk on the village green at Latimer records the service of four members of the Cavendish family and 11 other local men who served in the South African War.

73 The Earls of Oxford had given Chesham's tithes of corn (a tenth of a farmer's crop due to the church) and their right to appoint a vicar to Woburn Abbey. After the Dissolution, Woburn Abbey was acquired by the Earls of Bedford and their possessions in Chesham became known as the Manor of Chesham Woburn. The Earls of Bedford also purchased the neighbouring manor of Chenies. Members of the Russell family occasionally lived at Chenies Manor House until this century.

74 The Russell family constructed and still retain a chapel within the Church of St Michael, Chenies, where successive generations of the family are buried.

75 The oldest of the monuments in the Russell Chapel at Chenies is that of John, Lord Russell, created Earl of Bedford by Edward VI in 1550. He died in 1555 leaving instructions in his will for building the mausoleum.

76 The second manor called Cestreham belonged in 1066 to Edward the Confessor's widow, Queen Edith. It remained a separate manor known as Chesham Bury until 1486 when it was acquired by the Earls of Oxford, who already owned Chesham Higham. 'Bury' means 'fortified place' and the name seems to relate to the spur on which St Mary's Church stands. The house near the church, built in 1712 by William Lowndes, Secretary to the Treasury, was called The Bury, but is not the site of the original manor house.

77 An early owner of the Manor of Chesham Bury had given his half of the tithes and his right to appoint a vicar to the Abbey of St Mary de Pre, Leicester. In 1571 the Leicester property in Chesham, sometimes known as the Manor of Chesham Leicester or Chesham Leicester Rectory, was leased by the Crown to Thomas Ashfield, the Earl of Oxford's bailiff there. In 1579, Ashfield bought from the Earl the site of the manor house of Chesham Bury and some land including Cowcroft Farm in Botley. The Ashfields' house near the church was called Bury Hill or the Upper Parsonage and was probably on the site of the original Chesham Bury manor house.

78 The Ashfields sold Bury Hill to the Whichcotes, who sold it to the Skottowes. The ornamental lake in front of Bury Hill House became known as Skottowe's Pond. William Lowndes added Bury Hill to his own property in 1802 and demolished the house. The Lowndes family leased the pond and site of the house to Chesham Urban District Council in 1920, but retained the freehold until 1953.

79 This avenue of Dutch elms linking the Church to Blucher Street was the main feature of the grounds of Bury Hill House. The trees were cut down in 1950.

80 A third manor called Cestreham in Domesday Book can be equated with Chesham Bois. The manor belonged to a branch of the Cheyne family from the 15th to the 18th centuries, but their Manor House was destroyed and is evidenced only by foundations found in the garden of the early 19th-century Bois House.

81 There are several memorials to the Cheyne family in St Leonard's Church, Chesham Bois. The church looks modern owing to the thoroughness of the Victorian restoration including the addition of a tower in 1884.

82 The Manor of Chesham Bois was purchased in 1735 by John Russell, Duke of Bedford, who already owned Chenies and the manor of Chesham Woburn. The Russells sold the manor in 1903 to John W. Garrett-Pegge, whose neo-gothic Chesham House was then re-named Chesham Bois Manor. The architect was J. Wallis Chapman, who was later to design the Broadway Baptist Church. After its sale in 1978, the house was turned into a nursing home and the woodland either side of the Amersham Road was bought by the Woodland Trust.

83 There are several estates in Chesham which gained the status of separate manors before sub-infeudation was made illegal by a statute of 1290. Great Hundridge was a sub-manor of Chesham Higham. The lords of the manor in 1199 were the Le Broc family who came into conflict with the Abbot of Woburn regarding provision of a chaplain for their chapel which served Hundridge.

84 The dispute over the chapel at Great Hundridge was still running in 1504 when the Abbot of Woburn denied any obligation to provide a chaplain, saying that the chapel was so ruinous that no priest would dare to celebrate mass there. The building was converted into a barn and survives to this day as a billiard room.

85 Grove was another sub-manor of Chesham Higham, for its owners paid a chief rent of 13s. 4d. a year to the Earls of Oxford in the 13th century. This part of the manor house complex was in use as a barn when photographed in 1912.

86 Some historians have claimed (on insufficient evidence) that the surviving building at Grove was a chapel rather than a part of the manor house. The building was converted into a new house by the Harman family in 1970.

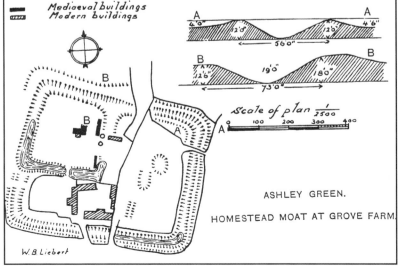

87 The Royal Commission on Historical Monuments prepared this 1912 diagram of the double moat which still surrounds the site of the manor house at Grove. The moat is up to 20 ft. deep and surrounds an area large enough for the owner to bring in his and his tenants' stock if threatened by soldiers or cattle thieves.

88 Another Chesham freehold which achieved the status of a manor was Blackwell Hall. This belonged to a William Blackwell in 1227. The manor was largely in the hamlet of Waterside and included a corn mill on the River Chess, later converted into a paper mill. The photograph shows Blackwell Hall around 1900.

89 St Mary's Church is cruciform with a central tower topped by a lead-covered wooden spire. It is difficult to date the stone and flint structure except by architectural features which may have been moved or heavily restored. Looking from the south east, we can see that the south windows of the chancel are of the Decorated style, dating from the 14th century, whilst the south window of the south transept is of the Perpendicular style and dates from the 15th century. The tower, which is supported internally on 13th- and 14th-century arches, has 15th-century windows in its upper stage.

90 The 15th-century porch has a fine stone vaulted ceiling. The room above is reached via a door in the south aisle and a spiral staircase which also gives access to the aisle roof. Note the huge block of pudding-stone under the buttress to the left of the doorway. It has been suggested that the pudding-stone blocks forming the foundations of the church are remnants of a pre-Christian stone circle.

91 Looking at St Mary's Church from the north we can see on the tower the outline of a steeply pitched roof to the north transept. The 15th-century north window of the north transept is Perpendicular in style.

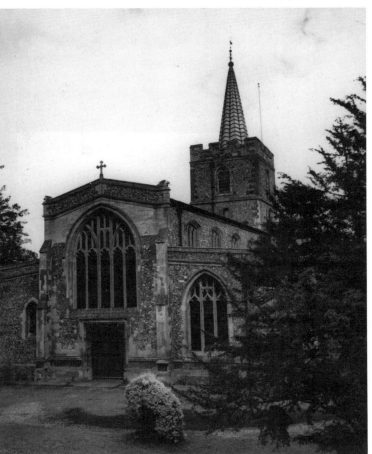

92 The huge five-light west window also dates from the 15th century when the nave was raised to accommodate the clerestory windows. The 13th-century single-light window in the north aisle also contrasts with the elaborate three-light window of the south aisle.

93 The west doorway is also from the 15th century. It has wide moulded door jambs and a flat four-centred arch. The carved oak doors are original.

94 The nave of the church is 64 ft. by 22 ft. The arcades of five arches on either side date from the 13th century when the north and south aisles were built. The jamb of a blocked Norman window can be seen in the north aisle.

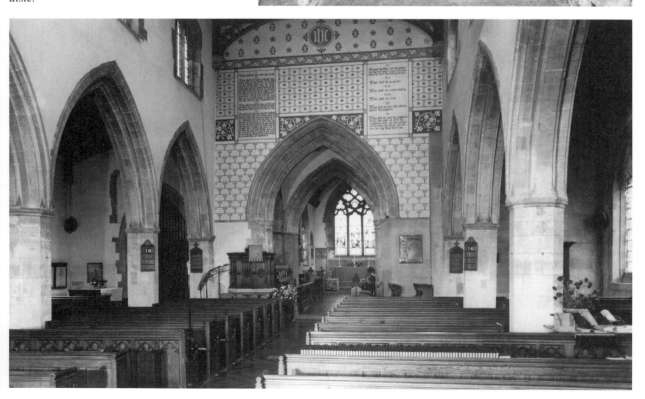

95 This Norman window, once giving light to the north transept, was blocked up when the north aisle was constructed.

96 The chancel is 35 ft. by 16 ft. The three-light east window is Victorian, dating from Gilbert Scott's restoration, but the north window is from the 14th century. Between them is a recessed bust of Richard Woodcoke, Vicar of Chesham from 1607 to 1623, who earned the nickname 'the hammer of heretics'.

97 In the south transept is this fine monument dating from 1617, commemorating the death of John Cavendish, son of Chesham's new lord of the manor, the Earl of Devonshire.

98 Chesham had one parish church but once had two vicars. Before the Dissolution, the Abbots of Woburn and St Mary de Pre, Leicester, took their respective tithes and each appointed a priest to officiate at Chesham. After the Reformation, the Earl of Bedford acquired the rights of Woburn Abbey and Thomas Ashfield purchased the Leicester interest. The two tithe owners continued to appoint their own vicars until the Duke of Bedford bought out his rival's rights and consolidated the living by Act of Parliament in 1767. From that date only one vicar was appointed. He occupied this new vicarage built by the Duke of Bedford within the churchyard.

99 The Church of England, worried by the success of nonconformist churches, particularly in industrial towns, devoted enormous resources to church building in the Victorian period. Chesham's expanding industrial district of Waterside was given its own church in 1864. Christ Church, Waterside was capable of seating 350 people. Further churches were built to serve the hamlet of Botley in 1871, Ashley Green in 1875, and the growing suburb of Newtown in 1887.

100 Long before the Reformation, there were those in the Church who desired freedom of conscience and the opportunity to read the Bible in their native language. Such independent spirits were called Lollards and several of their number in the Chesham area were persecuted for their beliefs. This stone cross in Chesham Churchyard was erected in 1908 to commemorate the burning at the stake of Thomas Harding of Chesham in 1532 at White Hill, where another memorial stone has been erected.

101 *(left)*   The spirit of nonconformity remained strong in the district and blossomed after the Civil War, when Oliver Cromwell allowed a large measure of religious freedom. He promoted a presbyterian or democratic form of church organisation. Many of the clergymen appointed during this period were ejected in 1662 after the restoration of the monarchy, but many presbyterian congregations continued in secret until licensed under the Toleration Act of 1689. The Presbyterians in Chesham, who later became Congregationalists, built this meeting house, set back from the Broadway, in 1724.

102 *(below)*   The old Congregational Meeting House was repeatedly extended but a completely new building fronting the Broadway was erected in 1885. The chapel was loosely based on the Early-English style of Gothic architecture and was designed by W.G. Habershon & Fawkner. It cost £2,859 and had 350 sittings.

103 Many dissenters embraced belief in believers' baptism. The Vicar of Chesham reported the presence of Anabaptists to his Bishop in 1669. After the Act of Toleration, Baptist congregations were able to organise effectively at area and national level. A group believing in the general redemption of all believers (General Baptists) built this meeting-house in Star Yard, off Broadway, in 1712. They were linked with meetings at Berkhamsted and Tring, forming one church.

104 The meeting-house in Star Yard was enlarged in 1735 and again in 1835, but remained tucked away until the present building was erected 1901-2. It was designed by J. Wallis Chapman and, with 900 sittings, is one of the largest nonconformist meeting-places in Buckinghamshire.

105 Beside the General Baptists of Bucks and Herts were some who embraced the Calvinistic belief in the redemption of 'particular' believers only. A Particular Baptist group at Chesham, linked with others at Watford and Hemel Hempstead, secured a licence in 1701 to hold services in a house formerly belonging to William Nash. They formed a separate church in 1707 and erected a meeting house in 1718 in an orchard behind a house in Red Lion Street belonging to Francis Sleap, a tailor and one of the original trustees. Sleap's house later became a beerhouse called the Punch Bowl, where the Brotherly Society of Tradesmen met. In this 1888 view, part of the meeting-house can be seen at the rear.

106 *(above left)*   The Particular Baptists extended their 'Lower Meeting' on several occasions, notably in 1797 and 1810, as well as adding a schoolroom in 1828. In 1888 they paid £900 for the site of the *Punch Bowl* to enable them to rebuild on the Red Lion Street frontage. A new chapel was not built on the site until 1897-8. It was designed by John Wills of Derby and had 520 sittings. The cost was £3,300. It was named the Hinton Baptist Church after the famous Baptist family who were members in the 18th and 19th centuries.

107 *(left)*   The Strict Baptists seceded from the Lower Meeting in 1820 and built this chapel in Townfield Yard. The chapel was sold in 1927 on the migration of the cause to Newtown Baptist Church and was used by Messrs. Griffin as a boot factory before its destruction by fire in the 1930s.

108 *(above)*   The Newtown Baptist Church in Berkhampstead Road, built in 1927, replaced the building in Townfield Yard. It was designed to hold 450 people.

109 Methodism does not have as long a history in Chesham
as in other industrial towns, owing to the early success of the
Baptists and Congregationalists. The present Chesham
Methodist Church has a continuous history from 1896; its
first chapel adjoined Gladstone Road. After the Wesleyan,
United and Primitive Methodists amalgamated in 1932, the
church acquired this building in Bellingdon Road. It had
been erected in 1907 as the United Free Church by seceders
from the Broadway Baptist Church. It was replaced by the
present Methodist Church in the 1960s.

110 The Salvation Army erected a Citadel in Broad Street
in 1898. The building is currently being renovated.

111 The various denominations vied with each other to educate Chesham's children. The tall building opposite the *White Lion*, Townfield Yard, was the British School, built by the nonconformists in 1828 with the assistance of the British and Foreign School Society, which is still represented on Prior's Educational Charity.

112 The Church of England fought back in 1845 with a new school in Church Street supported by the National Society for the Education of the Poor in the Principles of the Established Church. It was designed by the well-known church architect G.E. Street and is now used as St Mary's church rooms.

113 An infants' school in Germain Street was built in 1851 by the established church on the site of the old tithe barn. The 1902 Education Act passed control of church and board schools to the County Council. Germain Street School, rebuilt in 1911 as an elementary school, is now the Thomas Harding School.

114 In 1876, a school board of seven members was formed, empowered to raise local rates to pay for non-denominational schools. The first board school to be built in 1878 was at Townsend Road to educate the children from the new houses surrounding the boot and brush factories. After extensions in 1883 it was capable of housing 390 pupils.

115 Perhaps the best known of Chesham's board schools is Whitehill School, the multi-gabled building overlooking the railway station. It was built in 1890 and could accommodate 700 children. Although closed as a school in 1967, it became an adult education centre and, as the Chesham and District Community Centre, it is now the home of many of Chesham's societies.

116 Chesham has a creditable history of providing for its poor families. In 1624, Thomas Weedon, a draper and Citizen of London, left £500 to endow four almshouses in his native town. His trustees, 12 substantial householders, purchased a strip of land in the Forelands of the Town Field and built these almshouses according to Weedon's instructions. They applied the remainder to the purchase of 100 acres of land in the hamlet of Hundridge which produced a rent sufficient to repair the almshouses and to give the occupants a few shillings per week.

117 As a large and populous parish, Chesham had to provide a building where the poor who could not be maintained in their own homes were given shelter in return for their labour. This building on the corner of Germain Street is the earliest known workhouse in the town.

118 Weylands, with its fine 18th-century facade facing Germain Street, was Chesham's second parish workhouse. Under the 1834 Poor Law Amendment Act, Chesham was included in a union of parishes whose poor were accommodated in a new Union Workhouse in Amersham, designed by Gilbert Scott. The removal of the poor to Amersham in 1838 caused riots in Chesham.

119 *(above left)* Lace had been vital to the Buckinghamshire economy since the 16th century when parish overseers promoted its manufacture as a useful occupation for those deprived of work on the land and sold the finished goods to offset the poor rate. By 1792 there were four lace dealers in Chesham and lace was regarded by the *Universal Directory* as the town's premier industry.

120 *(above right)* When lace-making became less profitable in the 1820s, many dealers switched their labour force to the manufacture of straw plait for the Luton hat makers. By 1851 there were over 700 plait makers in the parish of Chesham. Here a former plait maker demonstrates the plait mill used to straighten and flatten the straw.

121 Many families were dependent on the earnings of female and child lace-makers and subsequently on those of the straw plaiters. In order to create more employment, a silk mill was built in Waterside about 1830 to employ Chesham's poor to spin yarn, which was woven into fabric at mills in other towns like Aylesbury and Tring.

122 The silk mill went out of business in the 1860s when duties were removed on foreign silks. The mill eventually became the Royal Bucks Laundry, which itself became a considerable employer of female labour.

123 The Royal Bucks Laundry erected this elegant new office block in the 1930s. With the advent of home washing machines, the laundry was forced to close down in the 1970s.

124 Chesham's position at the head of a valley led to its isolation from any through transport route. Not even the coach route down the Chess valley to Rickmansworth was turnpiked. The 'New Road' through Chesham Bois joining the Reading to Hatfield Turnpike at Amersham Common was, however, built about 1820. The old road winding through the woods behind Chesham Bois Manor can still be traced.

125 The London coach ceased in 1846 when services like this one from the *George Hotel* connected Chesham to the London & North Western Railway at Watford and Berkhamsted. Although more trains stopped at Watford, the station at Berkhamsted was nearer and drew more and more passengers and goods over the hill until Chesham secured its own railway in 1889. This photograph shows the Berkhamsted horse bus in the Broadway.

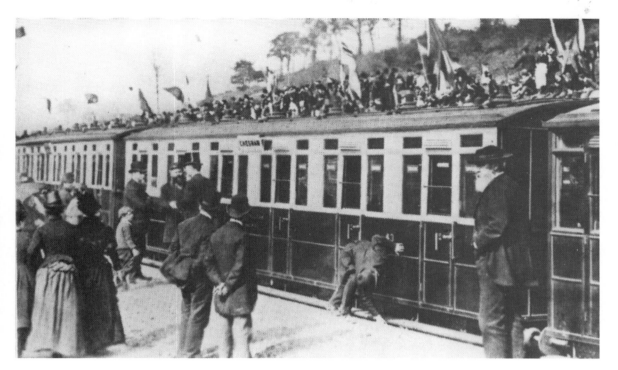

126 Many plans to bring railway lines from Amersham, Rickmansworth or Tring were abandoned before Chesham could celebrate the arrival of the first Metropolitan Railway train in 1889. The company purchased land to continue the line along the Vale towards Tring providing a loop line to London, but the 1892 line through Amersham to Aylesbury was to provide the more strategic link with the Great Central Railway.

127 Whilst Chesham manufacturers saw the railway as a means of getting their products to the capital, speculative builders saw it as an opportunity to sell houses in the countryside to London commuters. On the end of the platform in this 1897 view is an advertisement for valuable freehold building plots for the erection of villas.

128 *(left)* This photograph of the station in 1906 shows the boot factory of J. & E. Reynolds below the new houses on Stanley Avenue and Charles Long's factory beyond the cattle pens.

129 *(below left)* Another early view of the station shows the Chesham Brewery chimney in the distance.

130 *(below)* A new street, appropriately named Station Road, was laid out to link the station with the High Street. The *Chess Vale Temperance Hotel* was built on the corner.

131 The goods station was reached from White Hill. It was soon handling over 5,000 tons a month, coal being the bulkiest commodity.

132 The Chesham branch was steam powered until 1960. Here a former Great Central Railway 4-4-2 tank engine No. 67438 hauls the Chesham branch train on 20 July 1948.

133 Another ex-G.C.R. 4-4-2T No. 67418 about to leave Chesham with a train of three wooden coaches on 21 January 1955.

134 British Railways 4-4-2T No 67420 crosses the river Chess in May 1956.

135 The Chesham branch was electrified in August 1960. This view shows the third rail and one of the last steam-hauled trains waiting to depart.

136 The railway should have helped Nash's Brewery, which owned 11 of Chesham's pubs in 1872, to expand its trade. The brewery stood on the corner of High Street and White Hill. It was incorporated as the Chesham Brewery Ltd. in 1895 and in 1899 took over the rival brewery in Church Street run by Sarah How & Son. It merged with Hopcraft & Norris Ltd. of Brackley in 1947 to form the Chesham and Brackley Brewery and closed down in 1957.

137 Tanning was another local industry closely linked to the farming community. The largest tannery stood between the High Street and the vital stream running down from Higham Mead. The last operators were the Hepburn family who ran the tannery until its closure about 1850. Their fine house, later occupied by the Nash family, still stands in the upper High Street.

138 The other tannery, run in the 18th century by the Mead family, was situated on Germain Street, opposite Water Lane. It had a small bark grinding mill along Water Lane where the tannin used in the treatment of skins was produced. The tanner's house is still called The Meades.

139 Most market towns had shoemakers turning locally made leather into a product everyone needed. It was the proximity of the London market, however, which led to Chesham boot- and shoemakers to expand their production. Charles Long bought this baker's shop on the east side of High Street in 1883 and built a new boot factory behind.

140 Long later built three-storey offices and a showroom on the High Street frontage, but the project was not a success and the building eventually became the Co-operative Hall.

141 Another ambitious boot- and shoemaker, John Hayes, built this imposing factory at Waterside about 1890. It shared the same architectural features of Barnes' factory and those of the contemporary brush factories at Newtown.

142 John Hayes lived at The Thorns, a modest house next to the Waterside factory with a frontage on Amersham Road.

143 One of the biggest boot producers in Chesham was Reynolds Boot Factory in Blucher Street. The firm's sign can be seen on many turn-of-the-century views of Chesham.

144 Messrs. J. & E. Reynolds closed down in the 1920s and their factory and machinery was auctioned in 1930.

145 Messrs. Reynolds describe their employees in a 1908 article in the *Victoria County History*: 'The families engaged in the boot trade here are well paid and generally occupy good class cottages of the better order'.

146 One of the owners of the boot factory, Edwin Reynolds, was the first Chairman of Chesham Urban District Council. He built Broadlands House which was approached via a long driveway from White Hill. The house was later occupied by another boot manufacturer, George Barnes. New houses on Broadlands Avenue and Barnes Avenue now occupy the site.

147 Another Chesham boot and shoe manufacturer to apply modern machinery and mass production methods was George Barnes who built the Britannia Boot and Shoe Works in Addison Road, Newtown.

148 The interior of the Britannia Boot and Shoe Works, *c.*1900. George Barnes Ltd. continued until about 1980 when the firm merged with Giffard Newton & Sons of Townsend Road, the only surviving boot factory in Chesham today.

149 George Barnes was also elected to the first Chesham Urban District Council in 1894 and lived here at Britannia Villas on Berkhampstead Road.

150 The Chiltern woodlands afforded an abundant supply of beech wood for the manufacture of wooden tools and household goods. The wooden-ware manufacturers selected suitably fault-free timber in their own woods or on the estates of the larger Chesham landowners. This photograph of timber hauling was taken at Latimer in 1935, by which time high quality beech trees were becoming scarce.

151 Until the mid-19th century, the production of wooden articles was largely a cottage industry. Larger manufacturers perhaps employed a few journeymen turners in wooden sheds at the back of their houses. Stratford's Yard, to the east of Market Square, took its name from a wooden-ware manufacturer called Edmund Stratford. In 1851 the cottages were occupied by brush, hoop and shovel makers.

152 This late Victorian view of Waterside shows one of the first wooden-ware factories operated by Charles Grove, a wholesale wooden-ware manufacturer and turner. In the adjacent cottages, turners' wives would supplement the family income by plaiting straw for the Luton hat manufacturers.

153 Grove's factory can still be seen on this 1990 view of Waterside. It has since been demolished. On the left is Shackman's optical instrument factory and on the right the premises of H.G. Stone where the 'Hugmee' teddy-bears were made.

154 *(above)* With growing demand for wooden products from the London market, several wooden-ware manufacturers moved to purpose-built or adapted premises. In 1842, Thomas Wright established his business in a former bark mill approached from Germain Street via Water Lane.

155 *(above right)* Thomas Wright died in 1850 and his business was taken over by his son William. William Wright & Sons' extensive premises became known as the General Steam Saw Mills; its products included cricket bats, hoops, toy spades, sieve rims, brush backs, spoons, bowls and butter prints.

156 *(right)* William Wright & Sons closed down after a fire in 1968.

157 The former Bois Steam Mill in Amersham Road was converted into a wooden-ware factory about 1900 and used to make portable buildings and poultry houses. In 1920 it was renamed Canada Works and specialised in manufacturing pegs, mallets and other tent equipment. It is shown here in 1935.

158 The firm of James East & Sons was founded about 1860. With his sons Jesse and William he built a saw mill and workshops in Broad Street, opposite the Salvation Army Citadel, and directed the business until his death in 1925.

159 James East's grandson, Cyril Saunders, continued the business from its incorporation in 1930 until its closure in 1985. Here he is pictured next to a range of malt shovels produced by the firm, each of them made from a single plank of wood.

160   James East & Sons' timber yard backed on to Webb's Townsend Road brush works. It is pictured here about 1960.

161   Another well known Chesham wooden-ware manufacturer was Treacher Webb & Sons whose works were in Alexander Street, off Berkhampstead Road. The workmen are holding pick-axe handles but another speciality of the firm was the manufacture of wooden rims for bicycle wheels. During the First World War a Norwegian importer called Finn Sundt joined the firm, which later became known as Sundt & Co.

162 Chesham's premier wooden-ware manufacturer, Thomas Wright, began his business in Waterside in 1856. He was succeeded in the business by Jesse Wright, another of the original members of Chesham Urban District Council, who moved the firm to this new factory in Berkhampstead Road, Newtown, in 1910.

163 The interior of Thomas Wright & Son's works at Newtown. The workmen are manufacturing trundle hoops.

... hoops and seaside spades is despatched to the Metropolitan Railway station in 1914. Even ... could not compete with cheap imports of wooden ware from countries with abundant timber ... of business about 1963.

165 It was the nature of the wooden-ware trade that offcuts of timber could be used for other products. Brush backs were an obvious outlet and the manufacture of brushes became one of Chesham's staple trades during the second half of the 19th century. This photograph shows employees outside George Hawes' new brush factory in Higham Road in 1897.

166 The interior of George Hawes' factory, later to be known as 'Beechwoods'.

167 George Hawes' firm, dating from 1876, was incorporated in 1909 as Beechwoods Ltd. After a fire in 1930, the factory was reduced to two storeys. The firm was producing between 24,000 and 36,000 brushes a day in 1974.

168 Beechwoods had its own timber yard and saw mill in Higham Road. The firm closed down *c*.1980. It enjoyed worldwide goodwill, but had come to depend largely on imported materials.

169 Other members of the Hawes family did not join in the flotation of Beechwoods Ltd. in 1909. William Hawes set up his own brush factory in Cameron Road, which also suffered a serious fire. The factory was rebuilt on two floors instead of three.

The position of brush-making in Chesham
Webb, the son of a wooden-ware
who began his business here in the
1890s Robert Webb & Sons designed its
machines to produce domestic brushes and
employed 250 people.

171 *(above right)* Robert Webb's sons George and
William moved the firm to these new premises in
Townsend Road in 1889. From 1919, Webbs merged
with F. Foulger & Co. and concentrated on the
production of paint brushes.

172 *(right)* In 1948, a Huddersfield brush manufacturer
named Frank Jarratt joined the firm, which was then
known as Webb, Jarrett & Co. Ltd. After a series of
mergers in the paint brush industry, the Chesham factory
was closed in 1982 and production moved to the London
and Chepstow factories of the parent company, Brushes
International.

Walter ... of the ... der members of Chesham Urban District Council in 1894. William Webb lived ... here in Stanley Avenue. His neighbours included several of Chesham's nonconformist

174 The building of so many boot, brush and wooden-ware factories in Newtown led to a boom in house building along the valley. By 1900, Higham Mead, a source of the river Chess, was enclosed on three sides by houses lining Berkhampstead, Higham and Sunnyside Roads.

175 The connection to the capital via the Metropolitan Railway in 1889 caused demand for housing which has hardly abated in 100 years. New estates like these Chesham U.D.C. houses at Pond Park, pictured in 1937, threatened to transform the Chesham landscape, but a green belt policy has stabilised the population at about 20,000 and preserved the character of the town.

Bibliography

, Arnold. 'Chesham 100 Years Ago' in *Chesham Festival Souvenir*, 1951

, Arnold and Birch, Clive. *A Chesham Century*, 1994

, Arnold. 'The Lady Elgiva', in *Records of Bucks*, vol.25, 1983

, Arnold and Thomas, Anna. 'Latimer: the Mid-Fifth Century to the Present
' in Branigan, K., *Latimer*, 1971

, Clive. *Book of Chesham*, 1974

ighamshire County Council. *Chesham Town Map*, 1958

ighamshire Record Office. *Cavendish Estate Papers*

ighamshire Record Office. *Lowndes of Chesham Papers*

den, Pat. 'Chartridge and Pednor Hedgerows' in *Records of Bucks*, vols.28-9,

Valley Archaeological and Historical Society, *The People of Chesham*, 1984

, Clive. *The Chesham Shuttle*, 1996

-Pegge, W., *Transcript of the First Volume, 1538-1636, of the Parish Register*
1904

, George. *History and Antiquities of the County of Buckingham*, 1847

William d.). *Victoria History of the County of Buckingham*, 1905-27

, Pegg. *Whitehill School 1890-1990*, 1990

, Nikolaus and Williamson, Elizabeth, *Buckinghamshire*, 1994

Commission on Historical Monuments, *Inventory of the Historical Monuments
Buckinghamshire*, 1912-3

, J. J. *History and Topography of Buckinghamshire*, 1862

pton, R..., *Transcript of the 1851 Census Returns for Chesham*

tton, M. (ed.). *Latimer Remembered*, 1983

Index

Roman numerals refer to pages in the Introduction and arabic numerals to individual illustrations.